# Make Today Boldly Significant

*Fearfully and Wonderfully Me*
*Motivational Planning Journal Volume Two*

RIA STORY

Copyright © 2019 Ria Story

ISBN: 9781694020581

WHAT OTHERS ARE SAYING ABOUT RIA AND HER BOOKS:

*"I want to start by saying thank you…You made me want to try at life because you made me realize that you can make it anywhere you want, no matter where or what you are from. THANK YOU SO MUCH!"*JONATHAN, HIGH SCHOOL STUDENT

*"Ria's book (Beyond Bound and Broken) is full of hope and inspiration, and she shows us that despite experiencing horrific trauma as a young adult, that if we choose to, we can get past anything with the attitude that we bring to our life…Her book is full of wonderful quotes and wisdom."*
MADELEINE BLACK, AUTHOR OF UNBROKEN

*"I am using your material to empower myself and my female clients. Thanks for sharing your story and a wonderful journey of growth.*
'SUE QUIGLEY, LICENSED CLINICAL THERAPIST

*"Very few 'victims' would be willing to share such a personal story. However, nothing about Ria is average. She chose to rise above her painful past and now positions it in a way to offer hope and healing to others who've been through unspeakable abuse. Ria's faith and marriage keep her grounded as she reveals the solid foundation which helps her stand as an overcomer. Read this story and find yourself and your own story strengthened."*
KARY OBERBRUNNER, AUTHOR AND FOUNDER OF AUTHOR ACADEMY ELITE, ON *RIA'S STORY FROM ASHES TO BEAUTY*

*"Thank you, Ria, for bringing our conference to a close. You were definitely an inspiration to all of us! Awesome Job!"*
MELINDA, PRESIDENT AGS

"*Beyond Bound and Broken is a deeply inspirational book; one that will stay with you for years to come. The lessons are deep, yet practical, and her advice leads to clear solutions. This is a profoundly hopeful book. We all face pain, difficulty, and doubt but with resilience, we can lead vital, flourishing lives. Ria's story although sometimes painfully difficult to read because of the trials she endured is a story of great courage and compassion both for herself as victim and for those who betrayed her. Forgiveness is a strong theme as is courage. I would highly recommend this book to anyone who is struggling to move forward after experiencing a great trial.*" AMAZON CUSTOMER

"*...it was awesome! Ria has a real gift. I came away with so many helpful tools! Thank you, Ria.*" STEFANIE, CONFERENCE ATTENDEE

"*May God continue to bless your efforts. Your triumph is a great joy, and a gift to all that would hear or read it.*" LOUIS O., HUMAN RIGHTS ADVOCATE

"*What an inspiration you are to all of us especially the women audience. Your book is a clear example & step by step guide on how to become an effective leader. It is so easy to read and simple yet meaningful which is the beauty of this book.*" K. POONWALA, CUSTOMER SUCCESS MANAGER, ON *LEADERSHIP GEMS FOR WOMEN*

"*I was truly inspired by your presentation and the life lessons taught.*" JENNIFER, CONFERENCE ATTENDEE

# DEDICATION

Dear Reader,

In 2013, I made a decision to leave my career and pursue my calling. It wasn't an easy decision. I gave up the security of a regular paycheck and great benefits. I also resigned from the job I had worked very hard to get and had gone to college for 10 years to become qualified for. It was a great job in a great organization, and I considered myself successful, especially considering where I had started.

But, as Mark Twain said, "The two greatest days in life are the day you are born and the day you discover why." On August 14, 2013, I found my "why." With it came the realization I was more interested in making a difference than making a dollar.

In full transparency, it hasn't been easy.

There were some ramen-noodle-budget months. I went an entire year without a haircut. We sold our house, our cars, moved to an apartment, cashed in our retirement funds, trimmed all unnecessary expenses, and invested everything into ourselves and starting our speaking/training business. Mack and I have sacrificed much during our journey to be where we are today.

However, I would do it all again in a heartbeat. I would definitely do some things differently, better, or sooner, but I wouldn't hesitate to make the same decision again. Why? Why would someone give up a great career, good salary, good health insurance, and start their "career" completely over, losing $30,000 their first year in business, and giving up nearly everything in order to pursue speaking, writing books, and inspiring others? Why?

Today it was for you. In 2013, I had no idea I would be writing this dedication to you for this journal. But, I knew I wanted to make a bigger difference in the lives of others. Today, it's you.

"God will give you a double measure," someone once told me. "You don't understand, He already has." I replied.

It's true! Today, Mack and I are incredibly blessed, not only with material things but also by the rewards that come from the work we do. And so, this motivational planning journal is dedicated to YOU.

# CONTENTS

Make Today Boldly Significant

# A NOTE FROM RIA

Every one of us wants a life of meaning, achievement, and fulfillment. We all have hopes, dreams, and goals to become the best version of ourselves, and we all yearn to achieve our potential in life. The desire, or more accurately the *need*, to become the best version of ourselves is part of the human experience and the human story. Something inside you is shouting, "I want to reach my potential and become the person God created me to be."

We were created for a purpose. The greatest joy is realizing our purpose, and the greatest satisfaction is fulfilling it. We honor the gifts God gave us when we steward them well in answer to His calling.

Maslow's Hierarchy of Needs begins at the bottom with basic needs (food, water, and shelter) and progresses up the levels to the top (self-actualization). Only after each level of the hierarchy has been satisfied is it possible to move up. In other words, it's rather difficult, or perhaps impossible, to reach your God-given potential if you are scrambling each day to simply find food and a place to sleep. It's simply a matter of not being able to direct your energy toward fulfilling your calling if you are using that energy toward fulfilling the more basic needs.

Energy may never actually be lost, but time certainly is. And, *your* energy is finite just like your time on earth. Since you are reading this, you may not literally be scrambling to find food and shelter today. But figuratively, when we are unable to execute on the small daily disciplines, we are unable to fulfill the higher calling on our lives.

Consider the words of Hal Elrod, "Remember that who you're becoming is far more important than what you are doing, and yet it is what you're doing that is determining who you're becoming."

You can't "be all that you can be" until you master the basic discipline of daily choices. The greatest gap in the world is the gap between what we know we should do and what we do. How many times have you heard you should drink eight glasses of water every day and exercise at least three times a week? But, do you actually do it?

We don't fail to reach a goal because we are broken in some way, or there is something wrong with us. When a baby is born, we call it a miracle. We don't become any less miraculous as we age. We don't turn from miracle to mediocre by our 10th birthday. We aren't broken, just human.

We often have great intentions but lack the ability to execute. Something fun gets in the way, life happens, or unexpected problems get in the way of our priorities. And sometimes, we let inconsequential things get in the way of what we most need to do. Then, we get frustrated with ourselves, give up completely, and hope to do better tomorrow, next week, or next year.

And when that happens, we may never reach our goals or build our dreams.

**We somehow fail to reach our God-given potential either because we don't believe it's possible or because we are unwilling to make the sacrifices necessary to turn our vision into our reality.**

Let me assure you, it's possible. We are "Fearfully and Wonderfully Made"(Psalms 139:14), and God doesn't create mistakes, only miracles. I am "Fearfully and Wonderfully" me, just as you are "Fearfully and Wonderfully" you. God created each of us with potential. Transforming ourselves into the person who can reach our potential is up to us. Personal transformation is a process that occurs over time with consistent, intentional improvement and forward progress.

Let me also assure you: It's not going to happen by accident.

And, that's where the sacrifice comes in. We actually must do something different if we want life to be different. Vision alone isn't enough. We must take action.

Our lives are our stories, and we write a chapter every day by the actions we take and the choices we make. Each day we make the right choices, we build integrity by honoring the commitments we make to ourselves and to others and become more in alignment with who we were intended to be.

John C. Maxwell said it this way, "Every time we choose action over ease, we develop an increasing level of self-worth, self-respect, and self-confidence."

The key to reaching our potential is living life on purpose, with purpose, for a purpose. We must make every day matter. It's important to know what your priorities are, **but it's just as important to live them out each day.**

And when we do, we realize the power to make every day "boldly significant" is within us.

When I realized living life on purpose was the key to reaching my potential, I became rather single-minded about it. I still am.

The power of focus and living out my priorities has enabled me to achieve amazing things. Not because I'm special, but because the principles of intentional living, applied discipline, and consistent execution are.

Trust me, there's a wide gap between being a trafficking victim and becoming a TEDx speaker, author, and certified leadership trainer.

I left home at 19 to escape my abusive father. He started sexually abusing me at age 12 and was trafficking me to men he met on the internet by the time I was 18. Learn more about how I overcame my childhood and teenage years in my book, *Bridges Out of the Past: A Survivor's Lessons on Resilience.*

When I left home, I didn't have a car, any money, or even a high school diploma. My first job was waiting tables in a pizza restaurant for $2.13 an hour. I was proud to have it. But, I didn't want to stay there the rest of my career. I'm not a genius, but I knew the job of my dreams wasn't going to come find me at Pizza Hut.

Using the principles I'm sharing with you in this planning journal, I moved beyond my past and began creating my future.

I earned three degrees, including an MBA with a cumulative 4.0 GPA. I got married and became a step-mom. I taught elite level group fitness classes to inspire others to be healthy physically. I competitively raced mountain bikes, winning four state championships in two years. I had a great career as the director of compliance with responsibilities for over 6,000 policies and millions of dollars in Medicare appeals for a large hospital. I ran seven marathons. (26.2 miles is a long way to drive, much less to run!) I shared the stage with Motivational Speakers Les Brown and John C. Maxwell. I spoke at TEDx Wilmington Women. I wrote many books on leadership and personal growth. I shared my story to help others learn how to overcome obstacles.

And, my story is still being written. Yours is too. We can achieve nearly anything when we are willing to do what it takes. It's not easy, but it is possible. And most importantly, it's worth it. Stop waiting for the right time, a better time, or more time. Most often, we are the ones who get in our own way, and overcoming most obstacles in life is easy compared to overcoming ourselves.

In the words of my husband Mack, "Make it happen or someone else will. It might as well be YOU." If you want to get in touch, ask a question, or share a success story, E-mail me at: ria@riastory.com

# HOW TO MAKE TODAY BOLDLY SIGNIFICANT

Boldly Significant days are the days great leaders, teachers, parents, grandparents, coaches, speakers, healthcare professionals, human resource professionals, team leaders, supervisors, and anyone else who wants to make a positive difference in the life of someone else live for.

Maybe you've had the pleasure of having a "Boldly Significant" day in the past. A day where you know you touched the life, heart, mind, and soul of someone and left a positive impression. A day not about success for yourself but about significance for someone else.

A day lived on purpose is the key to a life lived with purpose. It begins with intentional thinking. It seldom, if ever, happens by accident. But, when you start each day with a significant mindset, you know your day will be more focused toward fulfilling your purpose, adding value to others, and building the legacy you will leave behind. Just a few minutes of intentional thought every morning will allow you to focus your energy, increase your influence, and make your day Boldly Significant!

There are four dimensions to life: Physical, Mental, Spiritual, and Relational. Each dimension needs nurturing because if we fail to steward one dimension of life properly, we will become unbalanced. This leads to "failures" in one dimension, which ultimately causes failures in other dimensions.

Think of the busy executive who never has time to exercise. He may be very successful at work (one part of the social/relational dimension of life), but his lack of exercise leads to a heart attack (the physical dimension of life). And, recovering from the heart attack, he realizes his marriage is crumbling because he is never home. Distracted by a difficult divorce, he loses focus on his job and misses a deadline for a client. One day he suddenly realizes his health is bad, his job is at risk, his marriage is over, and he experiences a spiritual crisis of faith. "Why me, Lord?" He asks, bitterly blaming God for the consequences of his choices.

Certainly, we don't cause all of our problems in life. Life is hard, bad things happen, and there will be challenges. But, we do create many of our problems just like we can create solutions to them.

Every day we make hundreds if not thousands of choices, some seemingly insignificant. Those choices, cumulatively, create our future. We make our choices, and then, our choices make us. We can choose our thoughts, mindset, attitude, values, and actions, but we cannot outrun the consequences of those choices, positive or negative.

This is simply how life works.

Good choices lead to increased influence with other people, improved circumstances, more options, more opportunities, and better results.

Poor choices lead to bad results.

Good choices begin with intentional thought, core values, and the discipline to stay true to them. You may not always get it right even when you try. But if you never try, you almost certainly won't get it right. As Hal Elrod said, "The degree to which you accept responsibility for everything in your life is precisely the degree of personal power you have to change or create anything in your life."

In his book, "The 7 Habits of Highly Effective People," Stephen R. Covey stated the first three habits of personal victory are: 1) Be Proactive, 2) Begin with the End in Mind, and 3) Put First Things First.

I like to think of these habits this way:

1) **Choices create freedom.**

   As a human being, I have the freedom to make choices. Though there is much I cannot control, regardless of what happens, I can *always* choose my response to what happens. Therefore, I am response-able which means I am responsible for the choices I make. The right choices create more freedom in the future.

2) **Vision inspires action.**

   As a human being, created by a divine God, I have a God-given purpose and gifts to fulfill that purpose. I'm "Fearfully and Wonderfully Me." Even if the vision isn't yet clear, I need to know the direction I want to go to get closer to the goal. Once I have a vision of where I'm going, it's much easier to be inspired in spite of distractions and take action in spite of obstacles.

3) **Execution requires discipline.**

   It's not enough to plan my priorities, I must execute based on my priorities. The secret here is setting small intentional goals to begin with in order to build integrity with myself. Much like my physical muscles get stronger with exercise, my mental discipline will also get stronger when exercised. Self-discipline means giving myself a command and following through with it *without making excuses.*

With big dreams and bigger goals, I quickly realized becoming highly effective wasn't going to happen by accident. I have juggled many hats over the years, including working multiple jobs, going to college, balancing family commitments, and trying to stay healthy, all at the same time.

I realized how much better my days, weeks, and months were when I lived them on purpose, with purpose, and for a purpose, so I started searching for a tool that would help me live with more intention and in alignment with the three principles above. I needed something that would help me with balance and to be more effective in every dimension of life.

I had in mind a planner or daily journal that was easy to use, simple to understand, and wouldn't take up too much time. I needed a place for reflections and a daily motivational thought or quote for personal growth (Mental dimension), a reminder to practice gratitude (Spiritual dimension), somewhere to list my healthy living plan for the day (Physical dimension), space to list my top priorities for the day in order to accomplish my goals and to increase my influence with others (Relational dimension).

I couldn't find one.

I've purchased many journals over the years. I've purchased various calendars, personal planners, wall calendars, desk organizers, daily timers, and I have five calendars on my iPhone, including two personal Google calendars, two for business, and one just to keep up with Mack. (Just for fun, I love to add things to his calendar!)

At some point, I gave up on finding exactly the right tool for me. I created a Word document on my computer with an outline that helped me set my top priorities for the day in each dimension of life.

That's how the idea for my "Motivational Planning Journal" series was born. I'm pretty sure I made the term up. But since what I was looking for apparently didn't exist, there wasn't a name for it either.

How do you use it? It's simple. Spend the first few

minutes of your day with your Motivational Planning Journal. Sit down and spend just a few minutes first thing every morning filling out two pages. Reflect and think about the quote. Then, complete each section. It's not complicated, but it is effective.

To become intentional, create an intentional habit. Our habits either serve us or enslave us. Trust me, this habit will serve you and serve you very well.

"I don't have time in the mornings," you may be thinking. Or, "I have too much to do."

A moment of truth: we make time for what's important to us. You might have to get up a little earlier, quit hitting the snooze button, or hide in the closet with a flashlight if all else fails.

Whatever it takes. A few minutes is not too much to commit to if you want to make your day Boldly Significant and create your legacy one choice at a time.

Make the commitment to make the first few minutes of your day the most productive, and the rest of your day will take care of itself.

Once you capture your intentions in your planning journal, it will be much easier to follow through. Keep your planning journal with you. Throughout the day refer back to your priorities, commitments, and remember what you are grateful for.

When your take out order is wrong at the drive through, pull out your planning journal and remember you can choose your response. Remind yourself that the right response will increase your influence while the wrong one will decrease it.

When you are tempted by chocolate donuts at the office, pull out your planning journal and remember your commitment for being healthy today was to have an apple instead of a donut.

And, when you have an occasional slip-up, don't throw in the towel. Pick yourself up, dust yourself off, and put away your excuses. Own it and then improve it.

Once the 60 days are complete, you may want to flip back to day one and see how far you've come. Celebrate your progress and then keep going.

There are several journals in the series. Each journal has different quotes and a different "theme" to appeal to different seasons of life. (Find a complete list of journals at https://riastory.com/journals)

Choose a theme of resilience if you are going through a tough time. Choose a theme of productivity if you are challenged with a big project in your life. Choose a theme of motivation if you are feeling a little down.

Using your planning journal every day will help you harness the power of affirmation and living on purpose. Doing this enables you to achieve more of what's truly important based on *your* priorities and values.

One last reminder: Saying "no" to less important things creates the space, time, and freedom to say "yes" to more important things. Now that you have identified your priorities and goals for the day, don't allow other things to derail you. It's easy to say "no" with a smile when you are saying "yes" to something bigger.

Here's to making today, and every day, Boldly Significant.

# *Daily Motivational Planning Journal Pages*

*"Significance is a choice that only successful people can make."*

~ Mack Story

Today I'm grateful for:


Reflections & Thoughts:

Leading Me Well - One thing I will do today to be physically healthier is to:

Make It Happen - Priorities Today:

1)

2)

3)

Influencing Others Well - I will intentionally add value or be kind to someone today by:

*"Look around you. Purpose is calling you from under rocks and in the hearts and souls of others. Someone out there needs you more than you need them."*

~ Lt. General Hal Moore

Today I'm grateful for:

Reflections & Thoughts:

Leading Me Well - One thing I will do today to be physically healthier is to:

Make It Happen - Priorities Today:

1)

2)

3)

Influencing Others Well - I will intentionally add value or be kind to someone today by:

*"Aspiring to greatness is easy, achieving it isn't."*

~ Ria Story

Today I'm grateful for:

Reflections & Thoughts:

Leading Me Well - One thing I will do today to be physically healthier is to:

Make It Happen - Priorities Today:

1)

2)

3)

Influencing Others Well - I will intentionally add value or be kind to someone today by:

*"It is never too late to be what you might have become."*

~ George Eliot

Today I'm grateful for:

Reflections & Thoughts:

Leading Me Well - One thing I will do today to be physically healthier is to:

Make It Happen - Priorities Today:

1)

2)

3)

Influencing Others Well - I will intentionally add value or be kind to someone today by:

*"How you do anything is how you do everything."*

~ T. Harv Eker

Today I'm grateful for:

Reflections & Thoughts:

Leading Me Well - One thing I will do today to be physically healthier is to:

Make It Happen - Priorities Today:

1)

2)

3)

Influencing Others Well - I will intentionally add value or be kind to someone today by:

*"I am willing to put myself through anything; temporary pain or discomfort means nothing to me as long as I can see that the experience will take me to a new level. I am interested in the unknown, and the only path to the unknown is through breaking barriers, an often painful process."*

~ Diana Nyad

Today I'm grateful for:

Reflections & Thoughts:

Leading Me Well - One thing I will do today to be physically healthier is to:

Make It Happen - Priorities Today:

1)

2)

3)

Influencing Others Well - I will intentionally add value or be kind to someone today by:

*"I'd rather attempt to do something great and fail than to attempt to do nothing and succeed."*

~ Robert H. Schuller

Today I'm grateful for:

Reflections & Thoughts:

Leading Me Well - One thing I will do today to be physically healthier is to:

Make It Happen - Priorities Today:

1)

2)

3)

Influencing Others Well - I will intentionally add value or be kind to someone today by:

*"If you cannot do great things yourself, remember that you may do small things in a great way."*

~ Napoleon Hill

Today I'm grateful for:

Reflections & Thoughts:

Leading Me Well - One thing I will do today to be physically healthier is to:

Make It Happen - Priorities Today:

1)

2)

3)

Influencing Others Well - I will intentionally add value or be kind to someone today by:

*"We make a living by what we get, but we make a life by what we give."*
~ Winston Churchill

Today I'm grateful for:

Reflections & Thoughts:

Leading Me Well - One thing I will do today to be physically healthier is to:

Make It Happen - Priorities Today:

1)

2)

3)

Influencing Others Well - I will intentionally add value or be kind to someone today by:

*"In truth, those who change the world start by changing themselves."*

~ Ria Story

Today I'm grateful for:

Reflections & Thoughts:

Leading Me Well - One thing I will do today to be physically healthier is to:

Make It Happen - Priorities Today:

1)

2)

3)

Influencing Others Well - I will intentionally add value or be kind to someone today by:

*"In your career, carve away everything that doesn't match your passion and competence, and you'll have the artwork of your life."*

~ Alan Weiss

Today I'm grateful for:

Reflections & Thoughts:

Leading Me Well - One thing I will do today to be physically healthier is to:

Make It Happen - Priorities Today:

1)

2)

3)

Influencing Others Well - I will intentionally add value or be kind to someone today by:

*"It is in defining moments that our legacy is shaped."*

~ Ria Story

Today I'm grateful for:

Reflections & Thoughts:

Leading Me Well - One thing I will do today to be physically healthier is to:

Make It Happen - Priorities Today:

1)

2)

3)

Influencing Others Well - I will intentionally add value or be kind to someone today by:

*"It is the greatest shot of adrenaline to be doing what you've wanted to do so badly. You almost feel like you could fly without a plane."*

~ Charles Lindbergh

Today I'm grateful for:

Reflections & Thoughts:

Leading Me Well - One thing I will do today to be physically healthier is to:

Make It Happen - Priorities Today:

1)

2)

3)

Influencing Others Well - I will intentionally add value or be kind to someone today by:

*"Let your name be remembered for the good you have done, the joy you have spread and the love you have shared."*

~ Mother Teresa

Today I'm grateful for:

Reflections & Thoughts:

Leading Me Well - One thing I will do today to be physically healthier is to:

Make It Happen - Priorities Today:

1)

2)

3)

Influencing Others Well - I will intentionally add value or be kind to someone today by:

*"A life lived in the shadows of the past is a life not fully lived."*

~ Ria Story

Today I'm grateful for:

Reflections & Thoughts:

Leading Me Well - One thing I will do today to be physically healthier is to:

Make It Happen - Priorities Today:

1)

2)

3)

Influencing Others Well - I will intentionally add value or be kind to someone today by:

*"Man is so made that whenever anything fires his soul, impossibilities vanish."*

~ Jean De La Fontaine

Today I'm grateful for:

Reflections & Thoughts:

Leading Me Well - One thing I will do today to be physically healthier is to:

Make It Happen - Priorities Today:

1)

2)

3)

Influencing Others Well - I will intentionally add value or be kind to someone today by:

*"One thing I know: the only ones among you who will be really happy are those who will have sought and found how to serve."*

~ Albert Schweitzer

Today I'm grateful for:

Reflections & Thoughts:

Leading Me Well - One thing I will do today to be physically healthier is to:

Make It Happen - Priorities Today:

1)

2)

3)

Influencing Others Well - I will intentionally add value or be kind to someone today by:

*"Passion is the spark that will ignite your soul and fuel your energy long beyond the point where you would have otherwise quit."*

~ Ria Story

Today I'm grateful for:

Reflections & Thoughts:

Leading Me Well - One thing I will do today to be physically healthier is to:

Make It Happen - Priorities Today:

1)

2)

3)

Influencing Others Well - I will intentionally add value or be kind to someone today by:

*"If you wish to be great, you must begin where you are."*

~ Russell H. Conwell

Today I'm grateful for:

Reflections & Thoughts:

Leading Me Well - One thing I will do today to be physically healthier is to:

Make It Happen - Priorities Today:

1)

2)

3)

Influencing Others Well - I will intentionally add value or be kind to someone today by:

*"The quality of our lives improves dramatically when we take pride in our work."*

~ Michael Josephson

Today I'm grateful for:

Reflections & Thoughts:

Leading Me Well - One thing I will do today to be physically healthier is to:

Make It Happen - Priorities Today:

1)

2)

3)

Influencing Others Well - I will intentionally add value or be kind to someone today by:

*"Significance is about making a difference instead of a dollar."*

~ Ria Story

Today I'm grateful for:

Reflections & Thoughts:

Leading Me Well - One thing I will do today to be physically healthier is to:

Make It Happen - Priorities Today:

1)

2)

3)

Influencing Others Well - I will intentionally add value or be kind to someone today by:

*"The goal in life is not to live forever but to leave something that does."*

~ Chris Hodges

Today I'm grateful for:

Reflections & Thoughts:

Leading Me Well - One thing I will do today to be physically healthier is to:




Make It Happen - Priorities Today:

1)


2)


3)



Influencing Others Well - I will intentionally add value or be kind to someone today by:

*"The highest reward for a man's toil is not what he gets for it but what he becomes by it."*

~ John Ruskin

Today I'm grateful for:

Reflections & Thoughts:

Leading Me Well - One thing I will do today to be physically healthier is to:

Make It Happen - Priorities Today:

1)

2)

3)

Influencing Others Well - I will intentionally add value or be kind to someone today by:

*"The measure of your life will not be in what you accumulate, but in what you give away."*

~ Wayne Dyer

Today I'm grateful for:

Reflections & Thoughts:

Leading Me Well - One thing I will do today to be physically healthier is to:

Make It Happen - Priorities Today:

1)

2)

3)

Influencing Others Well - I will intentionally add value or be kind to someone today by:

*"The price of greatness is responsibility."*
~ Winston Churchill

Today I'm grateful for:

Reflections & Thoughts:

Leading Me Well - One thing I will do today to be physically healthier is to:

Make It Happen - Priorities Today:

1)

2)

3)

Influencing Others Well - I will intentionally add value or be kind to someone today by:

*"To be successful, you must get results. To be significant, you must help others get results."*

~ Mack Story

Today I'm grateful for:

Reflections & Thoughts:

Leading Me Well - One thing I will do today to be physically healthier is to:

Make It Happen - Priorities Today:

1)

2)

3)

Influencing Others Well - I will intentionally add value or be kind to someone today by:

*"There is no passion to be found playing small—in settling for a life that's less than the one you are capable of living."*
~ Nelson Mandela

Today I'm grateful for:

Reflections & Thoughts:

Leading Me Well - One thing I will do today to be physically healthier is to:

Make It Happen - Priorities Today:

1)

2)

3)

Influencing Others Well - I will intentionally add value or be kind to someone today by:

*"Those who have a heart for serving others in some way will build influence far beyond those who expect to be served."*

~ Ria Story

Today I'm grateful for:

Reflections & Thoughts:

Leading Me Well - One thing I will do today to be physically healthier is to:

Make It Happen - Priorities Today:

1)

2)

3)

Influencing Others Well - I will intentionally add value or be kind to someone today by:

*"Those with passion do. Those without passion try."*

~ Kevin Hall

Today I'm grateful for:

Reflections & Thoughts:

Leading Me Well - One thing I will do today to be physically healthier is to:

Make It Happen - Priorities Today:

1)

2)

3)

Influencing Others Well - I will intentionally add value or be kind to someone today by:

*"Purpose is that sense that we are part of something bigger than ourselves, that we are needed, that we have something better ahead to work for. Purpose is what creates true happiness."*

~ Mark Zuckerberg

Today I'm grateful for:

Reflections & Thoughts:

Leading Me Well - One thing I will do today to be physically healthier is to:

Make It Happen - Priorities Today:

1)

2)

3)

Influencing Others Well - I will intentionally add value or be kind to someone today by:

*"Wanting to be someone else is a waste of the person you are."*

~ Kurt Cobain

Today I'm grateful for:

Reflections & Thoughts:

Leading Me Well - One thing I will do today to be physically healthier is to:

Make It Happen - Priorities Today:

1)

2)

3)

Influencing Others Well - I will intentionally add value or be kind to someone today by:

*"We all have the power to help many people, but do we have the courage to start with one?"*

~ Tom Telesco

Today I'm grateful for:

Reflections & Thoughts:

Leading Me Well - One thing I will do today to be physically healthier is to:

Make It Happen - Priorities Today:

1)

2)

3)

Influencing Others Well - I will intentionally add value or be kind to someone today by:

*"When I began to live on purpose, I discovered my purpose."*

~ Mack Story

Today I'm grateful for:

Reflections & Thoughts:

Leading Me Well - One thing I will do today to be physically healthier is to:

Make It Happen - Priorities Today:

1)

2)

3)

Influencing Others Well - I will intentionally add value or be kind to someone today by:

*"When we discover what we are willing to pay a price for, we discover our life's mission and purpose."*

~ Kevin Hall

Today I'm grateful for:

Reflections & Thoughts:

Leading Me Well - One thing I will do today to be physically healthier is to:

Make It Happen - Priorities Today:

1)

2)

3)

Influencing Others Well - I will intentionally add value or be kind to someone today by:

*"When we love something, it is of value to us, and when something is of value to us, we spend time with it, time enjoying it, and time taking care of it."*

~ Scott Peck

Today I'm grateful for:

Reflections & Thoughts:

Leading Me Well - One thing I will do today to be physically healthier is to:




Make It Happen - Priorities Today:

1)


2)


3)



Influencing Others Well - I will intentionally add value or be kind to someone today by:

*"Your purpose is a one sentence summary of how you make the world better."*

~ Ria Story

Today I'm grateful for:

Reflections & Thoughts:

Leading Me Well - One thing I will do today to be physically healthier is to:




Make It Happen Priorities Today:

1)


2)


3)


Influencing Others Well - I will intentionally add value or be kind to someone today by:

*"Your soul lights up with meaning when you help others take one step more toward their goals."*

~ Brendon Burchard

Today I'm grateful for:

Reflections & Thoughts:

Leading Me Well - One thing I will do today to be physically healthier is to:

Make It Happen - Priorities Today:

1)

2)

3)

Influencing Others Well - I will intentionally add value or be kind to someone today by:

*"A person who's happy will make others happy."*

~ Anne Frank

Today I'm grateful for:

Reflections & Thoughts:

Leading Me Well - One thing I will do today to be physically healthier is to:

Make It Happen - Priorities Today:

1)

2)

3)

Influencing Others Well - I will intentionally add value or be kind to someone today by:

*"Always remember when you are committed to a life purpose that is bigger than your problems, your problems become relatively insignificant and you will overcome them with ease."*

~ Hal Elrod

Today I'm grateful for:

Reflections & Thoughts:

Leading Me Well - One thing I will do today to be physically healthier is to:

Make It Happen - Priorities Today:

1)

2)

3)

Influencing Others Well - I will intentionally add value or be kind to someone today by:

*"Be fearless in pursuit of what sets your soul on fire."*

~ Jennifer Lee

Today I'm grateful for:

Reflections & Thoughts:

Leading Me Well - One thing I will do today to be physically healthier is to:

Make It Happen - Priorities Today:

1)

2)

3)

Influencing Others Well - I will intentionally add value or be kind to someone today by:

*"Declare a bold future into existence based on what's possible, not what's probable, based on what can be, not what has been."*

~ Amir Ghannad

Today I'm grateful for:

Reflections & Thoughts:

Leading Me Well - One thing I will do today to be physically healthier is to:

Make It Happen - Priorities Today:

1)

2)

3)

Influencing Others Well - I will intentionally add value or be kind to someone today by:

*"Don't ask what the world needs. Ask what makes you come alive and then do that. Because what the world needs is people who have come alive."*

~ Howard Thurman

Today I'm grateful for:

Reflections & Thoughts:

Leading Me Well - One thing I will do today to be physically healthier is to:

Make It Happen - Priorities Today:

1)

2)

3)

Influencing Others Well - I will intentionally add value or be kind to someone today by:

*"Each of us has a purpose for which we were created. Our responsibility - and our greatest joy - is to identify it."*

~ John C. Maxwell

Today I'm grateful for:

Reflections & Thoughts:

Leading Me Well - One thing I will do today to be physically healthier is to:

Make It Happen - Priorities Today:

1)

2)

3)

Influencing Others Well - I will intentionally add value or be kind to someone today by:

*"How we spend our days is how we spend our lives."*

~ Annie Dillard

Today I'm grateful for:

Reflections & Thoughts:

Leading Me Well - One thing I will do today to be physically healthier is to:

Make It Happen - Priorities Today:

1)

2)

3)

Influencing Others Well - I will intentionally add value or be kind to someone today by:

*"If we can't lead ourselves well, we don't deserve to lead others at all."*

~ Mack Story

Today I'm grateful for:

Reflections & Thoughts:

Leading Me Well - One thing I will do today to be physically healthier is to:

Make It Happen - Priorities Today:

1)

2)

3)

Influencing Others Well - I will intentionally add value or be kind to someone today by:

*"If we contribute to other people's happiness, we will find the true goal, the true meaning of life."*

~ Dalai Lama

Today I'm grateful for:

Reflections & Thoughts:

Leading Me Well - One thing I will do today to be physically healthier is to:

Make It Happen - Priorities Today:

1)

2)

3)

Influencing Others Well - I will intentionally add value or be kind to someone today by:

*"In every day, there are 1,440 minutes. That means we have 1,440 daily opportunities to make a positive impact."*

~ Les Brown

Today I'm grateful for:

Reflections & Thoughts:

Leading Me Well - One thing I will do today to be physically healthier is to:

Make It Happen - Priorities Today:

1)

2)

3)

Influencing Others Well - I will intentionally add value or be kind to someone today by:

*"Life is not easy for any of us. But what of that? We must have perseverance and above all confidence in ourselves. We must believe that we are gifted for something and that this thing must be attained."*

~ Marie Curie

Today I'm grateful for:

Reflections & Thoughts:

Leading Me Well - One thing I will do today to be physically healthier is to:

Make It Happen - Priorities Today:

1)

2)

3)

Influencing Others Well - I will intentionally add value or be kind to someone today by:

*"Memories of our lives, of our works, and our deeds will continue in others."*

~ Rosa Parks

Today I'm grateful for:

Reflections & Thoughts:

Leading Me Well - One thing I will do today to be physically healthier is to:

Make It Happen - Priorities Today:

1)

2)

3)

Influencing Others Well - I will intentionally add value or be kind to someone today by:

*"Passion in its purest sense, the willingness to suffer for what we love, is often the door that leads us to our path."*

~ Ralph Waldo Emerson

Today I'm grateful for:

Reflections & Thoughts:

Leading Me Well - One thing I will do today to be physically healthier is to:

Make It Happen - Priorities Today:

1)

2)

3)

Influencing Others Well - I will intentionally add value or be kind to someone today by:

*"Reading is to the mind what exercise is to the body and prayer to the soul. We become the books we read."*

~ Matthew Kelly

Today I'm grateful for:

Reflections & Thoughts:

Leading Me Well - One thing I will do today to be physically healthier is to:

Make It Happen - Priorities Today:

1)

2)

3)

Influencing Others Well - I will intentionally add value or be kind to someone today by:

*"Showing gratitude is one of the simplest yet most powerful things humans can do for each other."*

~ Randy Pausch

Today I'm grateful for:

Reflections & Thoughts:

Leading Me Well - One thing I will do today to be physically healthier is to:

Make It Happen - Priorities Today:

1)

2)

3)

Influencing Others Well - I will intentionally add value or be kind to someone today by:

*"There are no shortcuts to anyplace worth going."*

~ Beverly Sills

Today I'm grateful for:

Reflections & Thoughts:

Leading Me Well - One thing I will do today to be physically healthier is to:

Make It Happen - Priorities Today:

1)

2)

3)

Influencing Others Well - I will intentionally add value or be kind to someone today by:

*"To touch the soul of another human being is to walk on holy ground."*

~ Stephen R. Covey

Today I'm grateful for:

Reflections & Thoughts:

Leading Me Well - One thing I will do today to be physically healthier is to:

Make It Happen - Priorities Today:

1)

2)

3)

Influencing Others Well - I will intentionally add value or be kind to someone today by:

*"Too often, we underestimate the power of a touch, a smile, a kind word, a listening ear, an honest compliment, or the smallest act of caring, all of which have the potential to turn a life around."*

~ Leo Buscaglia

Today I'm grateful for:

Reflections & Thoughts:

Leading Me Well - One thing I will do today to be physically healthier is to:

Make It Happen - Priorities Today:

1)

2)

3)

Influencing Others Well - I will intentionally add value or be kind to someone today by:

*"What we leave behind when we die is a legacy footprint...the footprint of our lives."*

~ Ruth Tucker

Today I'm grateful for:

Reflections & Thoughts:

Leading Me Well - One thing I will do today to be physically healthier is to:

Make It Happen - Priorities Today:

1)

2)

3)

Influencing Others Well - I will intentionally add value or be kind to someone today by:

*"Your schedule should not be based on what you need to do, but rather what you want to become."*

~ Bill Hybels

Today I'm grateful for:

Reflections & Thoughts:

Leading Me Well - One thing I will do today to be physically healthier is to:

Make It Happen - Priorities Today:

1)

2)

3)

Influencing Others Well - I will intentionally add value or be kind to someone today by:

*"A job is printed on your résumé. A calling echoes in your epitaph."*

~ Dee Ann Turner

Today I'm grateful for:

Reflections & Thoughts:

Leading Me Well - One thing I will do today to be physically healthier is to:

Make It Happen - Priorities Today:

1)

2)

3)

Influencing Others Well - I will intentionally add value or be kind to someone today by:

*"Nothing great in the world has ever been accomplished without passion."*

~ Georg Wilhelm Freidrich Hegel

Today I'm grateful for:

Reflections & Thoughts:

Leading Me Well - One thing I will do today to be physically healthier is to:

Make It Happen - Priorities Today:

1)

2)

3)

Influencing Others Well - I will intentionally add value or be kind to someone today by:

*"One is not born into the world to do everything, but to do something."*

~ Henry David Thoreau

Today I'm grateful for:

Reflections & Thoughts:

Leading Me Well - One thing I will do today to be physically healthier is to:

Make It Happen - Priorities Today:

1)

2)

3)

Influencing Others Well - I will intentionally add value or be kind to someone today by:

# Check out more journals like this at RiaStory.com!!

**Make Today Ridiculously Awesome** (Motivational)
**Make Today Boldly Significant** (Purpose)
**Make Today Powerfully Productive** (Execution/Action)
**Make Today Joyfully Abundant** (Faith Based – Joy/Gratitude)
**Make Today Incredibly Beautiful** (Resilience/Overcoming Adversity)
**Make Today Extraordinarily Amazing** (Making the most of today)

# Excerpt from *PRIME Time: The Power of Effective Planning, by Ria Story*

I call it the *"whirlwind life."* You feel like you are living life in a tornado.

The vast majority of people in our society today are overcommitted, overstressed, overscheduled, too tired, and too busy. Most of them will tell you they don't like it.

Either, they don't know how to change it, or they aren't willing to. The former problem can be corrected by applying the principles in this book or by moving permanently to a deserted island where you are the sole inhabitant and completely cut off from all communication with the outside world.

The latter problem can only be corrected when the person *is* willing to change what needs to be changed.

Change isn't easy. It always requires more effort to make changes than it does to maintain the status quo. Changing your life is going to require energy, effort, self-discipline, and of course, time.

Work-life balance. It sounds good, like most lofty ideals do. But, how many of us have a good work-life balance? The term *"work-life balance"* assumes there is a life in there somewhere among all the work. However, for many of us, actually getting to the *"life"* part (or getting there with enough energy to enjoy it) is our biggest challenge. How often are you too exhausted by the end of the workweek to really enjoy Saturday morning spent with the kids because you are too busy catching up on laundry or working in the yard? There simply wasn't enough time to do your chores during the week. Or, you worked 10 plus hours per day at the office/job and still brought work home with you, so you could catch up.

Warning signs and symptoms that you may be experiencing the *"whirlwind life"* include: always running late or behind schedule, total exhaustion at the end of each and every day, forgetting commitments or appointments, and/or finding yourself unprepared for the day. Like the time I was 100% committed to going to the gym, but realized when I got there, I hadn't brought my sneakers.

The solution is simple. We need to manage time better, right?

Wrong. Nothing could be farther from the truth. In reality, no one can manage time. We can't buy it. We can't save it. We can't get it back. However, we can waste it. We can spend it. Or, we can invest it.

There is an entire industry focused on *"Time Management."* Millions of dollars are spent every year on planners, calendars, time tracking apps, and time budgeting software. There are literally hundreds of books on how to manage your time better, how to track where your time goes, and how to do it more efficiently. We hear phrases that sound great: *"Work-life balance"* or *"Manage your time, manage your life."*

Sometimes on the surface, the warning signs and symptoms seem easy to fix.

Does it sound too good to be true? It's not. It can be done. But, I won't promise it will be easy. If we want different results, we must do things differently. Making some of the changes in this book will require you to think deeply about what you truly want, what you truly value, and what you are truly willing to do to get it. You must be willing to make decisions, sometimes difficult decisions.

It won't happen overnight, and you won't get it right all of the time. None of us do. But, there is hope. So, stop waiting for the right time or a better time. Stop waiting for next year or soccer season to end. Stop putting off the important things in your life in order to do the pressing things.

This book is not for everyone. There are some people who will simply wish for life to be better or different but aren't committed to change. If you are looking for a quick-fix or an instant cure, this book is not for you.

Each section in this book has valuable information and a supporting exercise. Read the chapter. Then, complete the exercise. It's tempting to rush through the exercises or skip them entirely. You will get as much out of this book as you put into it. If you rush through the sections in an effort to get done, you will get very little from this book. Life likely won't change, and you will have simply spent some of your precious time wishing for life to be different or better instead of taking action to make it different or better.

The choice is yours – and as much as I would like to, I can't do it for you. You are the one in control of your life. Or, if you aren't in control of your life, you are the only one who can gain control of your life.

*It's your life.*
*It's time to stop going through the motions each day.*
*It's time to create the life you want.*
*It's time to stop trying to manage time.*
*It's time to start managing your life.*
*It's time to start leading yourself.*

## EXCERPT FROM *ACHIEVE: MAXIMIZE YOUR POTENTIAL WITH 7 KEYS TO SUCCESS AND SIGNIFICANCE,* by Ria Story

*"Character is the ability to meet the demands of reality."*

~ Henry Cloud

Integrity has four components: 1) Character; 2) Courage; 3) Commitment (to self); and 4) Congruency (with others).

Character is the foundational component because all the other components are built on top of character. In fact, integrity is determined by character. And, character is the determining success factor in life.

Your character and integrity determine how you will face life's challenges. Your response to success, failure, joy, pain, sickness, health, poverty, wealth, and the *"demands of reality"* will all be based upon your character.

Character is based upon intangible characteristics that will determine your success: attitude, work ethic, perseverance, resilience, discipline, courage, humility, and many more. Character is not based upon, or determined by, your education, background, race, ancestors, or experiences in life. Each and every day, you are writing your internal script by choosing your values. Then, your script (resulting character based upon the values you have internalized) will dictate your decisions and responses in any given situation.

Competency is your talent, natural gifts, skills, and abilities. Our character, not our competency, determines how far we will go and what we will ACHIEVE. Unfortunately, many people spend years developing their competency and little time developing their character and integrity.

In June 2013, I went to Guatemala on a mission trip. This wasn't a mission trip like you usually hear about where you take medical supplies and teach the Gospel. It was a mission trip to start the cultural transformation of Guatemala. This initiative had been years in the making because the President of Guatemala had asked John Maxwell for support in teaching the nation personal leadership principles.

While I was in Guatemala, our team trained various leaders; from Boy Scout troop leaders to top-level government officials. 150 coaches trained over 20,000 leaders in three days. One of the things we shared with them was 87% of who we are is determined by our character. The other 13% is what we know, our skills, knowledge and technical abilities. In other words, 87% of our success and influence comes from what we are, not what we know.

It's not always easy to live true to your values. Sometimes, having character requires you to face uncomfortable truths and stand up for what you believe. This happened to me early in my career.

I had recently been promoted to a new position in the organization where I worked. My new role was one of two identical positions in the organization. "Christy" (name changed) was my counterpart, and we had the same job duties and expectations. Christy had been there many years and had settled comfortably into her routine, so I knew I could learn from her.

I had a good work ethic, and I was eager to continue to make a good impression, hoping to continue moving up in the organization. Always a quick learner, I watched carefully how Christy did her job, and then I tried to see if I could make the process more efficient. I made some mistakes but quickly learned how to be more effective and efficient in my new role. And, I didn't mind working hard, taking initiative, and stepping up without being asked.

One day, my boss called me aside. *"Hey Ria,"* she said, *"Come here a moment."*

*"Sure,"* I replied, *"What do you need?"*

*"I've got a little problem,"* she chuckled, *"And, I need your help."* Always eager to help, I nodded for her to continue. *"Ok, sure."*

*"Everyone has noticed how quick you are learning, and you are really doing an outstanding job."*

*"Thank you!"* I smiled, excited she had noticed my efforts and hard work.

*"But the problem is, you are making Christy look bad. She's been here a lot longer and you are causing some problems for her. There are some concerns about why she doesn't do as good a job as you are doing. And, people are asking me why I let her get away with slacking off."*

I could feel my smile starting to melt. *"Oh?"*

*"Can you just slow down sometimes and try not to be so fast at your work? I don't mean you have to screw up on purpose but maybe wait until someone asks you before you do something that needs to be done."*

I couldn't believe it. My boss was telling me I needed to slack off because Christy didn't want to work hard.

I knew she and Christy were friends outside of work. They took trips together, went out for lunch, and even had drinks after work sometimes too. I also knew I wasn't going to slow down for one minute. I wasn't making Christy look bad, she was making me look good.

It put me in an uncomfortable position, but I told my boss I wasn't going to compromise my work ethic. And then, I showed her by continuing to work as hard as I could. Within two years, I had her job.

Character is having the right values. Integrity is living true to them. We must have the character to meet the demands of reality and the integrity to choose to do so.

# ABOUT THE AUTHOR

Like many, Ria faced adversity in life. Ria was sexually abused by her father from age 12 - 19, forced to play the role of his wife, and even shared with other men. Desperate to escape, she left home at 19 without a job, a car, or even a high school diploma. Ria learned to be resilient, not only surviving, but thriving. She worked her way through college, earning her MBA with a cumulative 4.0 GPA, and had a successful career in the corporate world of administrative healthcare.

Ria's background includes more than 10 years in administrative healthcare with several years in leadership and management including working as the Director of Compliance for a large healthcare organization. Ria's responsibilities included oversight of thousands of organizational policies, organizational compliance with all State and Federal regulations, and responsibility for several million dollars in Medicare appeals.

Today, Ria is a motivational leadership speaker, TEDx Speaker, and author of 13 books, including Leadership Gems for Women, and 6 Motivational Planning Journals. Ria is a certified leadership speaker and trainer and was selected three times to speak on stage at International John Maxwell Certification Events. Motivational speaker Les Brown also invited Ria to share the stage with him in Los Angeles, CA.

Ria has a passion for health and wellness and is a certified group fitness instructor. She has completed several marathons and half-marathons and won both the Alabama and Georgia Women's State Mountain Biking Championships in 2011 and 2012.

Ria shares powerful leadership principles and tools of transformation from her journey to equip and empower women, helping them maximize their potential in life and leadership.

# ABOUT MACK STORY

Mack began his career in manufacturing on the front lines of a machine shop. He grew himself into upper management and found his niche in lean manufacturing and along with it, developed his passion for leadership.

With more than 20 years working with and on the front lines, he brings a powerful blend of practical experience and leadership knowledge to his clients. Mack is a published author of several leadership development and personal growth books: Blue-Collar Leadership & Culture, Blue-Collar Leadership, Blue-Collar Leadership & Teamwork, Blue-Collar Leadership & Supervision, Blue-Collar Kaizen, Defining Influence, 10 Values of High Impact Leaders, MAXIMIZE Your Potential, MAXIMIZE Your Leadership Potential, Change Happens, Who's Buying You?, and 10 Foundational Elements of Intentional Transformation.

He understands that everything rises and falls on leadership.

For more detailed information on Mack, please visit TopStoryLeadership.com.

For information on Mack's unique Blue-Collar resources, please visit BlueCollarleadership.com

# Read more books by Ria

You have untapped potential to do, have, and be more in life. But, developing your potential and becoming the best version of yourself will require personal transformation. You will have to transform from who you are today into who you want to become tomorrow.

Ria Story brings unique insight in her book, "Fearfully and Wonderfully Me: Become the Woman You are Destined to Be" and the accompanying workbook to help you: believe in yourself and your potential; embrace your self-worth; overcome self-limiting beliefs; increase your influence personally & professionally; and achieve your goals & develop a mindset for success. These two resources will empower you to own your story, write a new chapter, and become the woman and leader you are destined to be.

# Order books online at Amazon or RiaStory.com

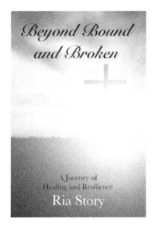

Ria Story

In *Beyond Bound and Broken*, Ria shares how she overcame the shame, fear, and doubt she developed after enduring years of extreme sexual abuse by her father. Forced to play the role of a wife and even shared with other men due to her father's perversions, Ria left home at 19 without a job, a car, or even a high-school diploma. This book also contains lessons on resilience and overcoming adversity that you can apply to your own life.

In *Ria's Story From Ashes To Beauty*, Ria tells her personal story of growing up as a victim of extreme sexual abuse from age 12 – 19, leaving home to escape, and her decision to tell her story

# Order books online at Amazon or RiaStory.com

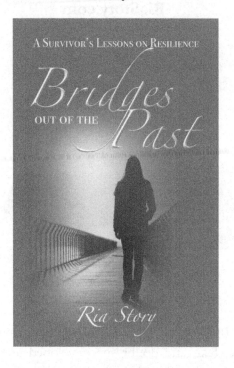

It's not what happens to you in life. It's who you become because of it. We all experience pain, grief, and loss in life. Resilience is the difference between *"I didn't die,"* and *"I learned to live again."* In this captivating book on resilience, Ria walks you through her own horrific story of more than seven years of sexual abuse by her father. She then shares how she learned not only to survive, but also to thrive in spite of her past. Learn how to overcome challenges, obstacles, and adversity in your own life by building a bridge out of the past and into the future.

*(Watch 7 minutes of her story at RiaStory.com/TEDx)*

# Order books online at Amazon or RiaStory.com

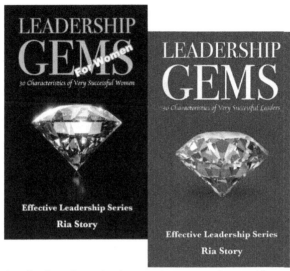

*Note: Leadership Gems is the generic, non-gender specific, version of Leadership Gems for Women. The content is very similar.*

Women are naturally high impact leaders because they are relationship oriented. However, it's a *"man's world"* out there and natural ability isn't enough to help you be successful as a leader. You must be intentional.

Ria packed these books with 30 leadership gems which very successful people internalize and apply. Ria has combined her years of experience in leadership roles of different organizations along with years of studying, teaching, training, and speaking on leadership to give you these 30, short and simple, yet powerful and profound, lessons to help you become very successful, regardless of whether you are in a formal leadership position or not.

## Order books online at Amazon or RiaStory.com

You have hopes, dreams, and goals you want to achieve. You have aspirations of leaving a legacy of significance. You have untapped potential waiting to be unleashed. But, unfortunately, how to maximize your potential isn't something addressed in job or skills training. And sadly, how to achieve success and find significance in life isn't something taught in school, college, or by most parents.

In *ACHIEVE: Maximize Your Potential with 7 Keys to Unlock Success and Significance*, Ria shares lessons to help you become more influential, more successful and maximize your potential in life. Three-page chapters are short, yet powerful, and provide principles on realizing your potential with actionable takeaways. These brief vignettes provide humorous, touching, or sad lessons straight from the heart that you can immediately apply to your own situation.

## Order books online at Amazon or
## RiaStory.com

Become inspired by this 30-day collection of daily devotions for women, where you will find practical advice on intentionally living with a grateful heart, inspirational quotes, short journaling opportunities, and scripture from God's Word on practicing gratitude.

# Order books online at Amazon or RiaStory.com

Ria's *Effective Leadership Series* books are written to develop and enhance your leadership skills, while also helping you increase your abilities in areas like communication and relationships, time management, planning and execution, leading and implementing change. Look for more books in the *Effective Leadership Series*:

- *Straight Talk: The Power of Effective Communication*

- *PRIME Time: The Power of Effective Planning*

- *Change Happens: Leading Yourself and Others through Change (Co-authored by Ria & Mack Story)*

- *Leadership Gems & Leadership Gems for Women*

## Order books online at Amazon or TopStoryLeadership.com

High impact leaders align their habits with key values in order to maximize their influence. High impact leaders intentionally grow and develop themselves in an effort to more effectively grow and develop others. These *10 Values* are commonly understood. However, they are not always commonly practiced. These *10 Values* will help you build trust and accelerate relationship building. Those mastering these *10 Values* will be able to lead with speed as they develop 360° of influence from wherever they are.

## Order books online at Amazon or BlueCollarLeadership.com

It's easier to compete when you're attracting great people instead of searching for good people.

*Blue-Collar Leadership® & Culture* will help you understand why culture is the key to becoming a sought after employer of choice within your industry and in your area of operation.

You'll also discover how to leverage the components of The Transformation Equation to create a culture that will support, attract, and retain high performance team members.

*Blue-Collar Leadership® & Culture* is intended to serve as a tool, a guide, and a transformational road map for leaders who want to create a high impact culture that will become their greatest competitive advantage.

**Down load the first 5 chapters FREE at:**
**BlueCollarLeadership.com/download**

## Order books online at Amazon or BlueCollarLeadership.com

Are you looking for transformation in your life? Do you want better results? Do you want stronger relationships?

In *Defining Influence*, Mack breaks down many of the principles that will allow anyone at any level to methodically and intentionally increase their positive influence.

Mack blends his personal growth journey with lessons on the principles he learned along the way. He's not telling you what he learned after years of research, but rather what he learned from years of application and transformation. Everything rises and falls on influence.

# Order books online at Amazon or BlueCollarLeadership.com

*10 Foundational Elements of Intentional Transformation* serves as a source of motivation and inspiration to help you climb your way to the next level and beyond as you learn to intentionally create a better future for yourself. The pages will ENCOURAGE, ENGAGE, and EMPOWER you as you become more focused and intentional about moving from where you are to where you want to be.

All of us are somewhere, but most of us want to be somewhere else. However, we don't always know how to get there. You will learn how to intentionally move forward as you learn to navigate the 10 foundational layers of transformation.

# Order books online at Amazon or TopStoryLeadership.com

*"Sales persuasion and influence, moving others, has changed more in the last 10 years than it has in the last 100 years. It has transitioned from buyer beware to seller beware"* ~ *Daniel Pink*

So, it's no longer *"Buyer beware!"* It's *"Seller beware!"* Why? Today, the buyer has the advantage over the seller. Most often, they are holding it in their hand. It's a smart phone. They can learn everything about your product before they meet you. They can compare features and prices instantly. The major advantage you do still have is: YOU! IF they like you. IF they trust you. IF they feel you want to help them. This book is filled with 30 short chapters providing unique insights that will give you the advantage, not over the buyer, but over your competition: those who are selling what you're selling. It will help you sell yourself.

# Order books online at Amazon or BlueCollarLeadership.com

**Are you ready to play at the next level and beyond?**

In today's high stakes game of business, the players on the team are the competitive advantage for any organization. But, only if they are on the field instead of on the bench.

The competitive advantage for every individual is developing 360° of influence regardless of position, title, or rank.

*Blue-Collar Leadership*® & *Teamwork* provides a simple, yet powerful and unique, resource for individuals who want to increase their influence and make a high impact. It's also a resource and tool for leaders, teams, and organizations, who are ready to Engage the Front Line to Improve the Bottom Line.

**Down load the first 5 chapters FREE at:**
**BlueCollarLeadership.com/download**

# Order books online at Amazon or BlueCollarLeadership.com

*"I wish someone had given me these books 30 years ago when I started my career on the front lines. They would have changed my life then. They can change your life now." ~ Mack Story*

*Blue-Collar Leadership® & Supervision* and *Blue-Collar Leadership®* are written specifically for those who lead the people on the frontlines and for those on the front lines. With 30 short, easy to read 3 page chapters, these books contain powerful, yet simple to understand leadership lessons.

**Down load the first 5 chapters of each book FREE at:**
**BlueCollarLeadership.com/download**

# Order books online at Amazon or
# BlueCollarLeadership.com

The biggest challenge in process improvement and cultural transformation isn't identifying the problems. It's execution: implementing and sustaining the solutions.

*Blue-Collar Kaizen* is a resource for anyone in any position who is, or will be, leading a team through process improvement and change. Learn to engage, empower, and encourage your team for long term buy-in and sustained gains.

Mack Story has over 11,000 hours experience leading hundreds of leaders and thousands of their cross-functional kaizen team members through process improvement, organizational change, and cultural transformation.

**Down load the first 5 chapters FREE at:**
**BlueCollarLeadership.com/download**

# Order books online at Amazon or TopStoryLeadership.com

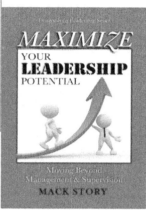

*"I wish someone had given me these books 30 years ago when I started my career. They would have changed my life then. They can change your life now." ~ Mack Story*

*MAXIMIZE Your Potential* will help you learn to lead yourself well. *MAXIMIZE Your Leadership Potential* will help you learn to lead others well. With 30 short, easy to read 3 page chapters, these books contain simple and easy to understand, yet powerful leadership lessons.

*Note: These two MAXIMIZE books are the white-collar, or non-specific, version of the Blue-Collar Leadership® books and contain nearly identical content.*

Make Today Boldly Significant

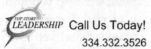
148

Made in the USA
Middletown, DE
28 February 2023